To

WE'RE GOING TO

FROM

....

INSTAGRAM: CREABOOKS

CREABOOKSPUBLISHINGS@GMAIL.COM

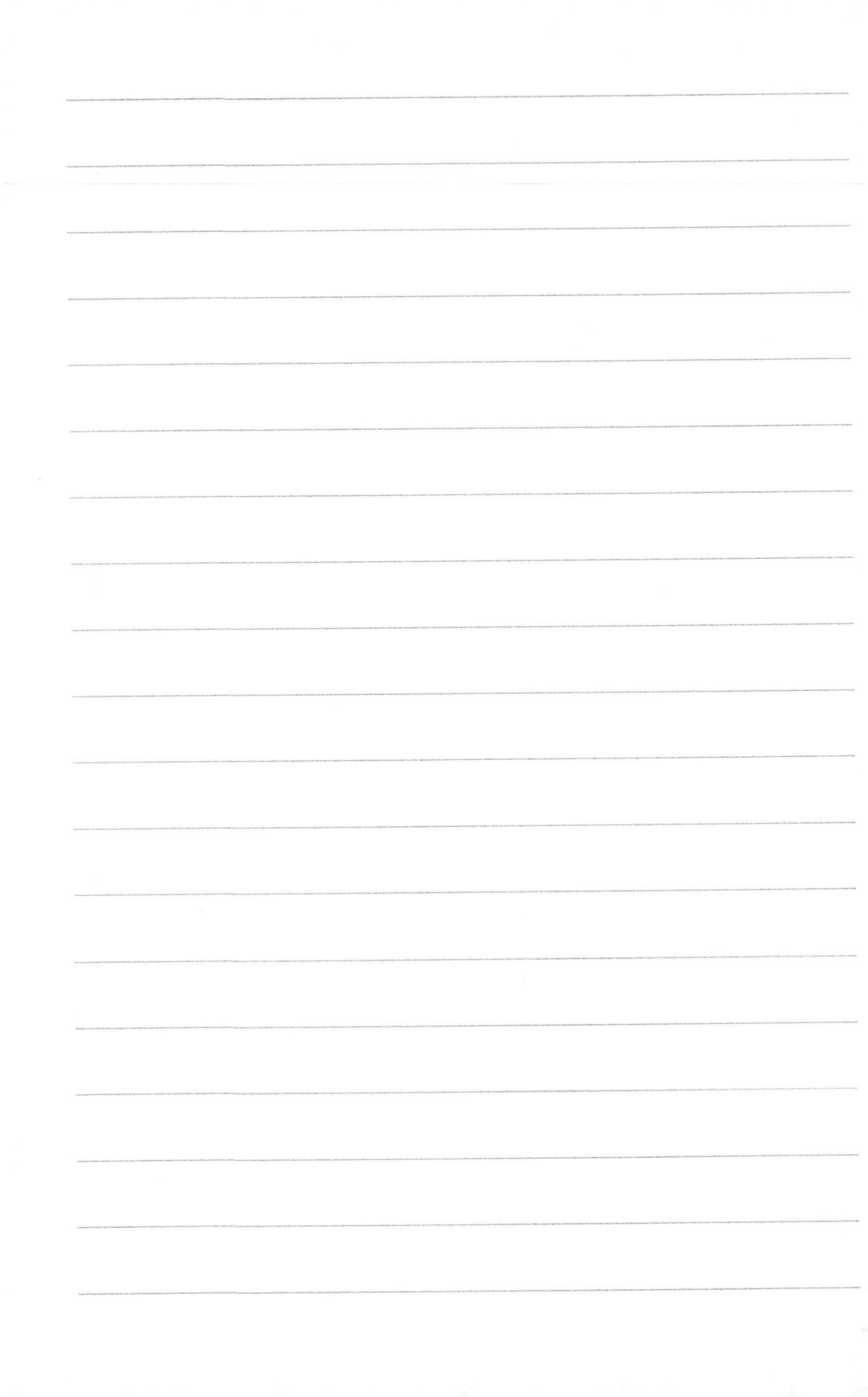

THANK YOU FOR PURCHASING!

WANT A FREEBIE?
LEAVE A REVIEW FOR YOUR AMAZON PURCHASE & CONTACT US VIA INSTAGRAM OR EMAIL!

CHECK OUT OUR HUGE RANGE OF BOOKS AT HTTP://TINY.CC/CREABOOKS

INSTAGRAM: CREABOOKS

CREABOOKSPUBLISHINGS@GMAIL.COM

Made in the USA
Coppell, TX
11 July 2025